Energizers

Calisthenics for the Mind

Carl Olson

71 Activities to Energize Your
School • Group • Organization
Club • Team

Published by

Educational Media Corporation®
P.O. Box 21311
Minneapolis, MN 55421-0311
(763) 781-0088 or (800) 966-3382
www.**educationalmedia**.com

ISBN 1-930572-07-7
Library of Congress Catalog No. 00-110153
Printing (Last Digit)

12   11   10   9   8   7   6   5   4

Production editor—
Don L. Sorenson, Ph.D.
Graphic Design—
Earl Sorenson

Energizers

About This Book

"Tell me and I will forget.
Show me and I will remember.
Involve me and I will understand."

The activities contained in this book are examples of experiential learning. I feel that using experiential techniques as a part of our regular teaching is the most effective way to achieve the level of understanding that we work so hard to attain. The advertising industry shows us the best examples of this. Ask any child to fill in the following statement: "Silly Rabbit, _____ are for _____." Any red blooded American young person who has watched television will quickly respond "Tricks are for Kids." We could think of many examples from advertising. One that comes to mind for me would be: L.S.M.F.T. You have to be near my age to respond to this, but the answer is Lucky Strike Means Fine Tobacco. I hate smoking! My father died from lung cancer! Yet I cannot remove this example of learning from my head.

How do the people in the advertising industry manage to accomplish this learning? They use many different types of media—visual, sound, print, music, and color—just to name a few. Wouldn't we like to have our students learn our material with that same intensity? I contend that complete learning will not happen with traditional chalk and talk instruction. Research shows us that only 10% of what we tell people is retained. If any other industry performed at only a 10% rate, it would soon cease to exist. For this reason, I advocate a multisensory approach, and experiential methods are the best way to accomplish this.

> *"The best learning is*
> *that which is self discovered."*
> **Carl Rogers**

There are many other benefits to the experiential approach. Cooperative learning is a very important outcome that we should be striving for in today's educational setting. I found the following quote in a newspaper recently:

> *"Today's workplaces need people who are*
> *flexible and adaptable, who have an*
> *intuitive ability to solve problems and work*
> *in teams, who are independent creative*
> *thinkers and can communicate effectively."*
> **Peter J. Pestle,**
> **Vice Chairman Ford Motor Corporation**

These qualities are what the world of work needs from its work force today and in the future. This will not happen in a traditional educational setting. Cooperative learning is a goal of the experiential process where students are required to work in a team setting to solve problems. In doing so, each individual student is able to contribute his or her personal strengths to the process.

Attention span is another area of concern that we try to address through this type of teaching. I have been very fortunate to teach at all levels during my teaching career. In middle school we have the 11-minute rule. Eleven minutes is the average attention span of a middle school student. From my elementary experience I know that their attention spans are considerably less, and I know the problem continues as students progress into high school. With effective teaching we must keep the idea of attention span in mind, and a good teacher has the ability to change gears in order to accommodate.

There is another important consideration—we need to "energize" the mind and senses before learning can effectively take place. In the this manual you will find many activities and exercises designed to jump start the learning process that are categorized in the three following classifications:

ENERGIZERS: Activities designed to activate the emotional nature of the group. The energizer can be directly related to the educational objective being presented or simply act as a mood enhancement vehicle. This type of activity is most often short and works well as an introduction tool.

GAMES: Organized play that includes competition on an individual or team basis. They can be related to an educational objective or be used as a team building tool.

INITIATIVES: Activities that go beyond games and energizers. They are exploratory in nature creating more in-depth analysis of thoughts, feelings, impressions, and reactions. In order for them to be effective, they must always be followed with processing questions.

Although I would like to take credit for creating these activities, I can only say that they have come to me through my varied education experiences and that I have found ways to make them work for me. Where these activities originated is unknown, but their uses and adaptations seem to be infinite. Additional excellent sources may also be found in the bibliography and resource list.

I have also included objectives for each of these activities. Although they are familiar and comfortable for me, I challenge you to adapt the materials for your own personal environment and goals. The beauty of experiential learning is the freedom you have in the creative use of these activities.

> *"Energizers are calisthenics for the mind.*
> *In order to have effective learning,*
> *we must activate the senses."*
>
> **Carl Olson**

Table of Contents

About This Book **3**
Introduction **9**

Energizers **13**

1	The Great Push Miracle	14
2	How Many Squares?	16
3	Ns and Ms	18
4	Number Sense	20
5	Adding Machine	23
6	Twenty-One	24
7	Birthday Surprise	26
8	Bloop	28
9	Air Bags	29
10	7 to 11	32
11	On Target	33
12	Animal Match	35
13	Look Beyond	37
14	Magic Squares	38
15	Mystery Cups	40
16	Pencil Trick	42
17	How Many Fs?	44
18	Peanut Butter & Jelly Sandwich	45
19	Start with a Bang	46
20	The Mall Game	47
21	Draw Me	48
22	If This Is, Is That?	50
23	On Your Mark, Get Set, Go!	52
24	Crack the Code	53
25	Rock, Paper, Scissors	55
26	Pig Personality Profile	56
27	Euclid's Triangle	58
28	12 Squares	59
29	Memory Tricks	61
30	Count Up	64

31   Photographic Memory 65
32   Comfort Zones 66
33   Thinking Outside the Box 67
34   Squaring the Square 69
35   Seasons of the Year 70
36   Be a Star 71
37   Nim 73
38   Look Up Look Down 76
39   The Big Wind Blows 77
40   Add'em 78
41   10 Nouns 79

Games **80**
42   Musical Chairs 81
43   Catastrophe 83
44   Zoom Erk 87
45   Electricity 89
46   Buzz 90
47   Balloon Train 91
48   Train Wreck 92
49   Four on a Couch 94
50   Elbow Tag 96
51   Gotcha 97
52   Zapper 100
53   Blind Tic Tac Toe 102
54   Tic Tac Toe Race 103
55   Name That Tune 104
56   Two Truths and a Lie 105
57   Who Am I? 107
58   Blanket Drop 108

Initiatives **109**
59   One-Way/Two-Way Communication 110
60   Broken Squares.. 114
61   If Eggs Could Fly 117
62   The Magic Dot 118
63   Reverse Pyramid 120
64   Random Numbers 121
65   Inclusion/ Exclusion 123
66   A Man Bought a Horse.................................. 125
67   Northwoods Survival....................................... 127
68   Headbands 131
69   Who Has the Answer? 134
70   Checkerboard Challenge 136
71   Pledge of Allegiance 139

About the Author **143**
Resource List... **143**

Energizers

Introduction

Education has been one of the loves in my life since 1968. After graduating from St. Cloud State University in St. Cloud, Minnesota, I eagerly accepted my first teaching position that fall. For the grand sum of $6,500 ($500 was for coaching), I set about teaching junior high physical education and health in Chetek, Wisconsin. During the ensuing years, I feel very fortunate to have been exposed to a multitude of special experiences that have shaped and driven me in directions that have kept my personal fire burning. In the twilight of my teaching career, I have been able to maintain my enthusiasm and I am thankful to the many people and organizations that have provided the fuel for my personal fire.

In particular, I would like to single out my wife of 31 years. Kathy is a kindergarten teacher. Watching her daily care and concern for her students is an inspiration for me. We have regular conversations about school that allow both of us to share what we do. Having a soul mate in the business allows us to get through the ups and downs of education. Kathy shares my enthusiasm for teaching and supports my work outside the classroom.

My sons Nick and Patrick and daughter Katie have provided their own special inspiration. It is difficult to minimize your importance when you have had daily insight to the effect of your profession on those you love. My children and I went through school together. I learned a great deal about what works and what doesn't by observing them. In recent years I have received a special bonus as our daughter has followed in our footsteps and is currently a middle school science teacher.

Outside of my family there have been many special influences. I do not have the time or the space to mention all of them, but I could not complete this section without special mention of some of the most important. Mr. Don Larsen, Executive Director of the Wisconsin Association of School Councils, has been a very special mentor. In his 70s, he runs our state organization. What we have at the WASC is very special and Don is the man who makes it go. So much of what I do and who I am comes from my WASC experiences. My special thanks to Don for his guidance and patience.

Dr. Earl Reum is the godfather of leadership educators. I feel fortunate to have had the pleasure of working with him for three summers. The National Leadership Training Center at Camp Cheley, Colorado provides a truly unique setting for developing future leaders and Earl was the heart and soul of the program. My favorite Earlism is this quote from P.T. Barnum:

"Make it big,
Do it right,
Give it class,
And wrap it with love."

Thank you Earl!

My list of individuals who have helped or influenced me could go on forever, but in addition to these individuals, there are also special organizations that I want to recognize. I have already mentioned the WASC. In addition to my relationship with Mr. Larsen, this organization brought me in contact with people who share my love of teaching and believe in the power of today's youth. The WASC continues to inspire me and is my best support group against burnout.

The NASSP (National Association of Secondary School Principals), and their affiliate organization, the NASC (National Association of School Councils), have provided me with experiences that are the icing on the cake. My camp experiences in Colorado and Florida will always be very special. These camps are special because of the students, teachers and staff members I had the opportunity to meet, work with, and share my enthusiasm.

I have had the opportunity to teach at all levels of the public schools and I know from this experience that each level has its own issues and makes its own important contributions. I have gathered these materials from my more than 30 years of educational experience. I know they work, and I also know that they will be user friendly for any teacher who truly knows children and likes working with them. Please use what you want and feel free to share any with others in our cooperative effort to make teaching and learning fun.

Energizers

1 The Great Push Miracle

Activity Type: Energizer

Group Size: Any number

Materials: A soda bottle and a piece of Kleenex

Time: 5 Minutes

Procedure: Start the class or group out by referring to what your goal or objective is for the day. Example: "Today we are going to begin our study of the living cell." Then note that you want to perform a miracle trick before you begin your study.

Take the Kleenex and tear a small hole in the center. The hole should be large enough to fit over the top of the bottle. Tell the class that you can push the bottle through the hole without further tearing the Kleenex.

You can continue by saying that you can push other objects through the hole, (i.e., a book, a chair, and even a person). Ask the class which object they would like you to work your magic on. You then proceed to stick your finger through the hole in the Kleenex and push whatever they have directed you to push.

At this point you will get groans and maybe some laughs. Move into your lessons using the concept of miracle and the attention and energy you have created.

Example: Explain that this was a trick and not a real miracle, but the things they are about to learn about the living cell have true miracle quality.

Processing Questions:

No in depth processing would be needed, as this is a short introductory activity designed to capture attention. After the point has been made, you would go directly to the educational objective of the lesson.

2 How Many Squares?

Activity Type: Energizer

Group Size: Any number

Materials: "How Many Squares?" (#2A) worksheet

Time: 10 to 15 minutes

Procedure: Hand out the worksheet and have the group count the number of squares they can find on an individual basis. Give about 3 to 5 minutes for the process. Then, have the group give their answers out loud.

Have the students combine into groups of 2 or 3 and have them share perceptions. Again give them 3 to 5 minutes and go through the same process again. Project the diagram using an over-head and go through the correct answer with the class. The correct number is 41. There are 40 squares in the drawing and the word "square(s)" is in the title—40+1=41. You can add a 42nd if you copy the activity page on a square sheet of paper.

Processing Questions:

1. Why did we get so many different answers on the first trial?

2. Why was it helpful to work with other people?

3. How can we put this to work for us in everyday life?

Carl Olson

2A How Many Squares?

Individual Answer: _____

Group Answer: _____

3 Ns and Ms

Activity Type: Energizer

Group Size: Any amount

Materials: None

Time: 15 to 20 minutes including processing

Procedure: Start with the following question: In the United States are there more states that begin with the letter M or N? Give them one minute to come up with their answer. (This should be done on their own.) Poll the group to see if they believe the answer should be M or N.

At this point have them pair up with another person and share their answers. Poll the groups again and see what the results are. Have the pairs group with another pair and repeat the process. (The actual answer is that there are an equal number of Ms and Ns (8).)

Processing Questions:

1. How many people had the correct answer the first time?

2. What was the benefit from sharing your answer with another person?

3. How does what you learned apply to your:

   a. school work?

   b. social groups? (teams, clubs, etc.)

   c. future jobs?

Carl Olson

3A Ns and Ms

4 Number Sense

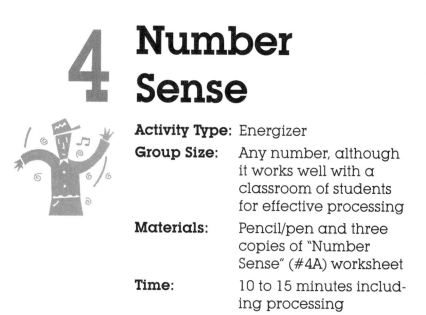

Activity Type: Energizer

Group Size: Any number, although it works well with a classroom of students for effective processing

Materials: Pencil/pen and three copies of "Number Sense" (#4A) worksheet

Time: 10 to 15 minutes including processing

Procedure: Pass out the first of three number sheets and have the students draw a line connecting the numbers in order. This is a timed event. Give them one minute to do as many as they can. After a minute, stop and have them compare their answers to see how many numbers they were able to locate.

Discuss what they think would happen if they were given another try.

Pass out another number sheet and give them a second chance. At this point have the students fold their sheet the long way so that there is a crease down the middle of the paper. Repeat the numbering activity again giving the students the same one-minute time period.

Discuss what they see about the arrangement of the numbers. They will find that the order of the numbers will follow a consecutive pattern. The odd numbers are all on the left hand side of the page and the even numbers are all on the right hand side of the page.

Give the students a third and final try. They should have the best results on this attempt because of the new information they have gathered.

Processing Questions:

1. What is a disadvantage to doing a task without information?

2. What is gained by doing the activity a second time? (practice)

3. How does additional information affect your results?

4. How does this exercise relate to your

   a. school work?

   b. life decisions?

4A Number Sense

① 53 16 54

27 39 15 28 40 6

51 5 2 26 52

13 17 41 14 50 30

29 3

37 25 38 4 42

49 18

55 36

7 23 46 34

31 12

43 22

35 19 44 24

11 57 8

32 58

45

47 33 20 60 56

21 9 59 48 10

5 Adding Machine

Activity Type: Energizer

Group Size: Any amount

Materials: None

Time: 10 to 15 minutes including processing

Procedure: Have the students pair up and face each other. Ask them to put one hand behind their backs where they will extend any number of fingers from one to five. On the signal of "go," they are to present their hidden hand with the selected number of fingers showing.

The winner is the first person to correctly add and announce the total number of fingers shown by themselves and their partner.

Processing Questions:

1. What are some benefits from competition? (fun, social interaction, mental stimulation)

2. What are some problems with competition? (stressful, time consuming)

3. In this competition, what was the one thing each person knew? (their own total of fingers)

4. How does this relate to life decisions?

6 Twenty-One

Activity Type: Energizer

Group Size: One to classroom size

Materials: None

Time: 10 to 15 minutes including processing

Procedure: Instruct the group that you will challenge individuals in a counting contest. One student is selected from the group to compete against you, the facilitator. The game involves counting to 21 and the object is to not be the person to say the last number (21).

Ask your opponent whether they would like to start the game or would they like you to start. The counting can be by ones or by twos. For example, if you say the number 1, your opponent can say 2 or 3. If your opponent chooses 3, you may say 4 or 5.

The trick to the game is that you will know the numbers that you need to control in the game in order to win. These numbers include: 2, 5, 8, 11, 14, and 17. (The numbers go up by threes after the number two.) If you are able to gain control of these numbers as you play, you will always win. If your opponent selects any of these control numbers, continue to try to control the numbers yourself. If you get the number 17, you will never lose. For example, a game could play out as follows, with you starting first:

You	Opponent
2	3
5	7
8	9
11	12
14	16
17	18
20	21

I like to use activities like this to change the pace of any group with which I am working. I can start a lesson with the activity, use it as a break when working on longer projects, or end with it. In all cases I am trying to get the group's attention and focus. When an individual student discovers the trick to the game, he or she feels empowered and you will have a special connection with that student.

Processing Questions:

None needed.

7 Birthday Surprise

Activity Type: Energizer

Group Size: Any number, works best with classroom

Materials: Birthday Surprise (#7A) overhead

Time: 10 to 15 minutes

Procedure: Make a transparency copy of the "Birthday Surprise" sheet (7A) and place it on an overhead projector in front of the group. Ask one student to think of the number of the day he or she was born. Then ask if the number is contained in column number one. Have that person say "yes" or "no." Repeat this for each of the five columns. Make a mental note of the top number in each of the "yes" columns. Add these top numbers in your head and they should equal the number of the day your volunteer was born. Continue this with other students. Tell the group that you will show them how the trick works after they complete their work for the day.

Processing Questions:

1. What were your thoughts as we first did this trick?
2. Does this system work for everyone in the room?
3. Why is it important to know how a system works?
4. What are some common systems that we use in everyday life?

Carl Olson

7A Birthday Surprise

1	2	4	8	16
3	3	5	9	17
5	6	6	10	18
7	7	7	11	19
9	10	12	12	20
11	11	13	13	21
13	14	14	14	22
15	15	15	15	23
17	18	20	24	24
19	19	21	25	25
21	22	22	26	26
23	23	23	27	27
25	26	28	28	28
27	27	29	29	29
29	30	30	30	30
31	31	31	31	31

8 **Bloop**

Activity Type: Energizer

Group Size: Any number. For larger groups you would need sub groups of 6 to 8

Materials: One balloon for each sub group. It should be blown up and tied

Time: 15 to 20 minutes

Procedure: Divide the students into groups of 6 or 8 people and have them disperse so that each group has space to work and they are not too close to another group. The members of each group should hold hands throughout the entire activity. The group's goal is to keep a balloon in the air using the following directions:

1. Heads only
2. Head and shoulders
3. Hands (or heads and hands)
4. Knees and feet

NOTE: I have them try to keep it up for 21 consecutive hits.

Processing Questions:

1. What was the mood of your group as you were doing the activity?
2. Is it possible to have fun and accomplish a task?
3. Did anyone try to dominate your group?
4. Is there a danger in this happening?

Carl Olson

9 Air Bags

Activity Type: Energizer

Group Size: Any number—works best with 6 or more

Materials: Two air bags—
Wren Enterprises
3145 West Monmouth Ave,
Englewood, CO 80110
303-748-2778

Time: 10 to 20 minutes

Procedure: The entire outline and sequence is on the Air Bags worksheet (#9A). The visual effect of this activity is very strong.

Processing Questions:

1. What did I do differently than the volunteer?
2. Why was my way more efficient?
3. Name some resources we need to use to be successful in life, school, sports, and so forth.

9A Air Bags

Objectives:

1. To energize and heighten student interests.
2. To give a visual symbol of the concept of successful cooperation.

Procedure:

1. Ask for a student volunteer.
2. Get the volunteer's name and let that person know that you are going to ask him or her to blow up a balloon. (Give the volunteer a chance to opt out at this point.)
3. After you have an agreement, unfold the air bag balloon and instruct the volunteer to blow it up while you talk. (Make sure to have the volunteer hold the air bag close to his or her mouth.)
4. While the volunteer is working, talk to the group, making the following points:
   a. We need to get adequate information before making a quick decision.
   b. It is also important that we know if the task we undertake is possible with the resources we have.
5. Show the class that the end of the bag is open so it is impossible to blow it up.
6. Suggest a contest between the volunteer and yourself. Tie the ends of the bags. Stand back to back and have additional volunteers holding the bags out horizontally from the contestant's mouths. "Ready, set, go" command and start the contest.

Carl Olson

NOTE: The secret move would have you holding your bag away from your face and blowing directly at the bag opening. If done correctly, you should fill the bag with one breath. Close the end and hold your full bag while the volunteer puffs away. (This will bring a big laugh from the observers.)

7. Thank the volunteer. Have that person sit down and ask the following questions.

Processing Questions:

1. Why is it important to know and understand what you are asked to do? (blow up a balloon)

2. Why is it important to understand if our task is achievable? (Relate it to increasing time pressure in their lives; also relate it to their ability to use their time to be successful as students, club members, etc.)

3. What did I do differently? (ANSWER: I held the balloon away from me.)

4. Why did this work better? (ANSWER: I used my breath and the surrounding air to accomplish the task.)

10 7 to 11

Activity Type: Energizer

Group Size: Any number. Have a large group make subgroups of three. If they do not come out even, you can have some groups of four.

Materials: None

Time: 15 to 20 minutes

Procedure: Form subgroups and have them face each other with one hand behind their backs. On the instructions of "go," have them hold up from 1 to 5 fingers. (*NOTE*: No obscene gestures.) In order to win, the total number of fingers on the three hands must total 7 or 11.

NOTE: No planning or external communications are allowed. Do the activity in sets of five. Do two to four sets.

Processing Questions:

1. Did you get better as the game went on?
2. Which number was the hardest to make?
3. What steps did your group go through to improve performance?

11 On Target

Activity Type: Energizer

Group Size: Small group to class-room size

Materials: Five envelopes with drawings inside. Four will be blank or have question marks. One will have a bull's-eye or target.

Time: 5 to 10 minutes

Procedure: This activity uses the magic principle of forced choice. Pick five helpers to hold the envelopes. (You know which one has the target.) Have one of the remaining students try to pick the correct one.

Ask one student to select two of the envelopes. If he or she picks the correct one, have the students holding those two envelopes step forward. If the correct one was not one that was chosen, have the two they picked step back.

Now, if you have it down to two, ask the student to pick one. If he or she chooses the right one, you are at the finish. If not, have that person step back, and you are still done.

If you were left with three, have a student pick two and repeat the process. To finish, you have all but the chosen one open their envelopes. Make a point about not wanting to be uncertain as we do today's work. Have the chosen person open up the envelope to reveal the target. Now make the point that we want to be on target in all that we do.

Processing Questions:

1. What was the purpose of using this activity?
2. Does the point I made fit with what we are trying to accomplish?
2, How can we use these ideas in the future?

12 Animal Match

Activity Type: Energizer
Group Size: Any number
Materials: None
Time: 15 – 20 minutes

Procedure: Have the group members pair up and stand back-to-back. Give them three different animals they can choose from. See the following page for suggestions and photos. Use these three or make up your own.

Count to three and have the pairs turn and face each other showing one of the animal signs. If they match, they have won the game. If they do not match, they must go again.

Repeat again with another partner. They can also group into 3s, 4s or any other number.

Processing Questions:

1. What happened to the group's mood when we did this activity?
2. What were the problems anticipating your partner's symbol?
3. What feelings did you and your partner have when you were successful?
4. How did it feel to be unsuccessful?
5. How is this communications process similar to everyday life?
6. What special problems did we have when we increased the number of participants?

Couch Potato

Elephant

Moose

13 Look Beyond

Activity Type: Energizer

Group Size: Any number. Works well with a regular class-room.

Materials: 10 to 15 objects that can be laid down and displayed. (example—paper clips, tooth picks, coins and so forth)

Time: 15 to 20 minutes

Procedure: Tell the students you are going to make patterns with the objects that will represent numbers from 0 to 10. (Ahead of time you will contact one group member to tell that person the solution.) Make a pattern. Tell the other group members what it is or write it on a sheet of paper. The person with whom you are working will turn around while you are doing this. When you are ready, have your partner turn and look at pattern.

NOTE: The pattern means nothing. The answer is in the number of fingers you are indirectly showing to the person you are working with on the trick. People will concentrate on the patterns you create, but the answer is in the finger positioning you are indirectly displaying. Thus the name "hands down."

Processing Questions:

1. How did you go about solving the problem?
2. What feeling did you have as other people figured it out?
3. What clue helped you to figure this out?
4. Why is it important to look beyond what you see?

---

14 Magic Squares

Activity Type: Energizer

Group Size: Six to classroom size.

Materials: Nine sheets of paper or make an overhead of the attached drawing (#14A).

Time: 15 to 20 minutes

Procedure: I use this activity as an interest enhancer. In this activity you need to select and prepare a helper ahead of time. See the attached sheet for instructions.

At the end of my first class I suggest that I have special powers to read people's minds. Before this class I have selected a student from each class to help me. The rest of the class does not know that I have met with the selected person. We do the mind reading demonstration and end it with the idea that there is a code we are using and the selected class member has vowed not to reveal it before our next class.

Processing Questions:

1. What ideas did you use in the solution of the problem?

2. What was it like to be the helper?

3. Which clue brought the solution to you?

4. Did all students get the solution at the same time?

Carl Olson

14A Magic Squares

Description:

1. Lay the nine squares out in the following pattern:

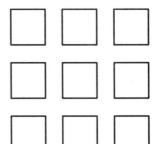

2. Have the selected person turn back around.

3. Ask one of the other students to pick any of the nine squares.

4. Have the selected person turn around and go through the squares until we reach the chosen one.

5. I will use a signal on the first square I point to and tell which one it is.

6. The first square is to be thought of as all of them—if I touch it at point #2, we are looking for #2 and so on. Each number point stands for the nine squares.

X	X	X
X	X	X
X	X	X

15 Mystery Cups

Activity Type: Energizer

Group Size: Any number

Materials: 3 plastic, paper, or foam cups

Time: 10 to 15 minutes

Procedure: This is a trick/stunt designed to create interest.

Place three cups as shown in the starting position of the diagram. Select a volunteer and have that person watch you demonstrate the three steps that it takes to get the cups in the down position. In step one use your right hand to flip cup "B" up and your left hand to flip cup "A" down. This should be done in one movement. In step two use your right hand to flip cup "C" down and your left hand to flip cup "A" up. In step three use your right hand to flip cup "B" down and your left hand to flip cup "A" down.

At this point, reverse the middle cup and challenge the volunteer to duplicate what you did. The trick is that this makes the starting set up different with cup "A" and "C" down and cup "B" up. Your hope is that the volunteer will not notice the difference and will not be able to come up with the same result.

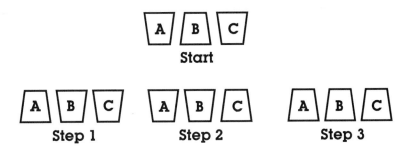

After you have finished and everyone understands, have them go home and try the trick on someone they know. Ask them to report back on the experience the next time you get together.

Processing Questions:

1. At what point did you figure out the trick of this activity?
2. What did it feel like to know the answer while others were still struggling?
3. How did it feel to be in the opposite situation?
4. Are there situations in our daily lives that are similar to this?

16 Pencil Trick

Activity Type: Energizer

Group Size: Any number

Materials: One pencil or pen (or similar shaped object) for each person. See the next page for a demonstration.

Time: 5 to 10 minutes

Procedure: Demonstrate the pencil trick for the group. Have them all try it. Bring individuals forward to try it. Walk them through it slowly. Finally leave the activity and challenge the group to work on it.

Notice in the pictures of the trick that the pencil moves from above the fingers to below and the hands do not cross over.

Processing Questions:

1. How hard did you think it would be to do when you first saw me do it?

2. How did you feel when you first attempted it?

3. Did anyone figure it out? If so, what helped you?

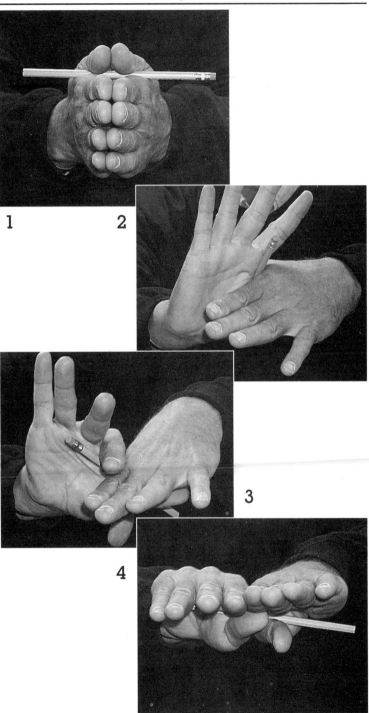

1   2

3

4

17 How Many Fs?

Activity Type: Energizer

Group Size: Any number

Materials: A copy of paragraph below for each participant

Time: 5 to 10 minutes

Procedure: Handout the "How Many Fs?" worksheet and challenge the group to count the number of Fs in the paragraph.

Poll the group to see what everyone got for answers. You should get a variety of answers. Have the group members pair up to compare answers. Poll the group again to see if the answers change.

Processing Questions:

1. Why did we get different answers the first time?
2. How did working with another person help?

How Many Fs?

**FINISHED FILES ARE THE
RESULTS OF YEARS OF
SCIENTIFIC EVIDENCE
COMBINED WITH
THE SHARING OF
DISCOVERIES.**

---

18 Peanut Butter & Jelly Sandwich

Activity Type: Energizer

Group Size: 5 to 30

Materials: Bread slices in plastic bag, knife, 1 jar of peanut butter, 1 jar of jelly, cleanup materials

Time: 10 to 20 minutes

Procedure: Ask the class for a volunteer. If several people are interested, choose one by any method (picking numbers, drawing names, and so forth.)

Have the chosen person turn away from you and give you instructions on how to make a peanut butter and jelly sandwich. As the directions are given, do exactly what is said. Use your imagination to foul up the process. (If the person says to put the peanut butter on the bread, put the jar of peanut butter on the bread.)

The class or group will get a kick out of this process. You can have other people replace or help the chosen person and get the same results.

Processing Questions:

1. Why did this activity go the direction that it did?

2. What was it like to be the person doing the explaining?

3. How is this activity similar to their life situations?

19 Start with a Bang

Activity Type: Energizer

Group Size: Any number

Materials: More balloons than there are people in the group

Time: 10 to 15 minutes

Procedure: Give every participant a balloon and ask them to blow them up and tie them off. Establish a boundary that you want them to stay within. Have each person in the group start batting his or her own balloon in the air and keep it in the air by batting it. Once they have started, have people outside the boundary throw in extra balloons. Keep doing this for 2 to 3 minutes.

Tell the group that as the balloons fall, they should try to get as many as possible back up. After the 2 to 3 minutes, have the group stop and sit down. At this point stress the following:

1. When we had one balloon, we were doing our thing.

2. As we tried to keep them in the air, we were working together.

3. As we added in more balloons, it was like adding work to be done.

Lastly, have them all stand up and stomp the balloons. We did this because we want to start with a bang. Have them pick up the broken balloons to show that we always clean up our messes.

20 The Mall Game

Activity Type: Energizer

Group Size: 10 to 30

Materials: None

Time: 15 minutes

Procedure: Memory experts tell us that association is one of the best ways to help us remember important information. This exercise uses that same principle to remember names.

Seat the group in a circle. Then, one at a time, have all of the members give their first name and an item they would go shopping for at the mall, (i.e., Carl—cars). Each person gives his or her own information repeats the previous ones in order.

This is most effective when the class knows each other and the teacher/leader/facilitator needs to learn their names.

After all the group members have given their information, it works well to scramble the group by playing "The Big Wind Blows." (See page 77.) After the group is well scrambled, test the leaders knowledge using names and shopping items.

Processing Questions:

1. Why is it difficult to remember names?
2. Why is it important to remember names and facts about members in your group?
3. How does association help to remember?

---

21 Draw Me

Activity Type: Energizer

Group Size: Any number—works very well with a classroom size group

Materials: Pencil and "Draw Me" worksheet (#21A)

Time: 20 minutes

Procedure: Give all participants a pencil and a "Draw Me" sheet. They should also have a clipboard or magazine for drawing. At the signal to start, all of the participants will circulate in the room, introducing themselves to and exchanging drawings with other people in the group. At each exchange, they draw one part of the other person's face.

The face parts are listed and the person doing the drawing signs for the part drawn. This activity is carried on until most of the drawings are completed. The facilitator should observe and encourage the process. After the drawings are complete, have the students sit in a circle and show their drawings.

Processing Questions:

1. How many in the group are not comfortable with their art ability?

2. How did it feel to draw someone?

3. How did you feel about your drawing?

21A Draw Me

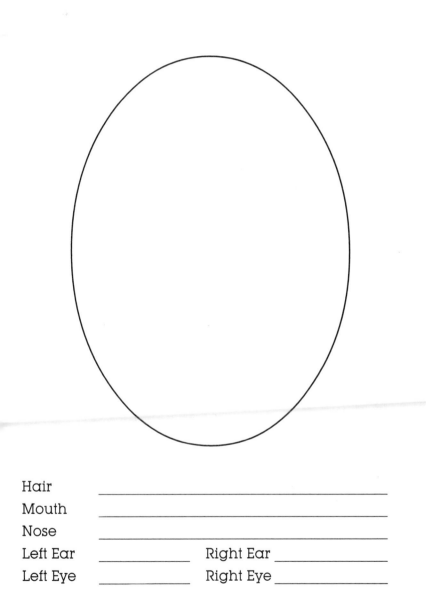

Hair   _____

Mouth   _____

Nose   _____

Left Ear   _____   Right Ear _____

Left Eye   _____   Right Eye _____

22 If This Is, Is That?

Activity Type: Energizer
Group Size: Any Number
Materials: None
Time: No Limit

Procedure: This is a riddle type activity. Begin by asking the group to try to solve a riddle. Ask them to keep the answer to themselves once they discover it. I use activities like this to open or close lessons or group work. They work well to fill time and keep the group interest level high.

The riddles ask the following series of questions:

If this is a _____,
and this is a _____,
is this a _____ ?

You need to pick out any three objects or things that are the same, (i.e., pencils, fingers, books, etc.). The key is how you start the process. If you just start the riddle as listed above, the answer will always be "no." However, if you start by saying "now listen," the answer will be "yes."

For example, if you ask the group: "If this is a book (pointing at a science book), and this is a book (pointing at a math book), is this a book (pointing at an English book)? The answer to the riddle would be, "no."

If you asked the same riddle in this way: "Now listen, if this is a book, and this is a book, is this a book?" The answer would be, "yes." "Now listen," is the signal that answer to the riddle is yes.

Carl Olson

Processing Questions:

1 At what point did you figure out the riddle?

2 What did it feel like to be in on the secret?

3 Are there times in daily lives where we have understanding of concepts while others do not?

23 On Your Mark, Get Set, Go!

Activity Type: Energizer
Group Size: Any number
Materials: None
Time: 5 minutes

Procedure: Ask for and select a group volunteer. Bring the volunteer to the front of the room and say that you are going to ask that person to race you. After he or she agrees to race, say the words: "On your mark, set, go!"

At this point you should have a confused person. You have not defined what type of race or where the race is heading. If you want, bring up another person and say the same words. Once again there will be confusion for the same reasons. Next have the volunteers sit down and process the situation.

Processing Questions:

1. What is wrong with what I am asking for?
2. What information would I need to provide to make this work?
3. How does this result relate to real life situations?

Carl Olson

24 Crack the Code

Activity Type: Energizer

Group Size: Any number

Materials: "Crack the Code" (#24A) worksheet

Time: 10 to 15 minutes

Procedure: Hand out the "Crack the Code" worksheet. Start with problem number one. Ask the group to imagine what the next figure would be in the sequence. Have them work individually at first. If any student thinks he or she has the correct answer, have he or she show it to you.

After some time with individual work, have them combine in small groups (2 or 3 members). Give the following hints as time passes:

pairs • numbers • back-to-back

For problem number two use the same system. Individual work followed by group work. Use the following clues for this exercise:

letters • curved/straight

NOTE: The answer to #1 is 88, each figure is a double number back-to-back. The answer to #2 is all letters with all straight lines go below the line and letters with curved lines go above the line.

Processing Questions:

1. Why was this difficult when you first tried it?
2. Did it help to work in groups?
3. Which clue helped you the most?
4. How does working in groups and getting clues relate to daily life?

24A Crack the Code

1. What should be the next symbol in the sequence?

2. What should the rest of this sequence look like?

```
 BCD  G
______________________
A   EF
```

25 Rock, Paper, Scissors

Activity Type: Energizer

Group Size: Any number—I have done this with more than 200.

Materials: None

Time: 5 to 10 minutes with processing

Procedure: Have your group stand and set up a game of Rock, Paper, Scissors. The rules are as follows:

1. If you win or tie, you remain standing.
2. If you lose, you have to sit down.

Play 4 to 5 rounds. Repeat the game for three rounds, but this time show the group what your symbol will be. In these cases the group members should always win when they know what your symbol is.

Processing Questions:

1. What was the difference between the two games?
2. Why is it important to be aware of what is going on?
3. What are some things we can do to increase personal awareness?

26 Pig Personality Profile

Activity Type: Energizer

Group Size: Any number

Materials: Pencil/pen, pieces of paper for each group member

Time: 10 to 15 minutes

Procedure: Follow the instruction as listed on the "Pig Personality Profile" (26A).

NOTE: The last example is only for adult groups. ONLY!

Processing Question:

None.

The act of completing the drawing and reviewing the analysis serves as the processing.

26A Pig Personality Profile

On a blank piece of paper, draw a pig. Don't look at your neighbor's pig. Don't even glance!

If your pig. . .

- ✔ Is toward the top of the paper, you are a positive, optimistic person.
- ✔ Is toward the middle of the paper (top to bottom), you are a realist.
- ✔ Is toward the bottom of the paper, you are pessimistic and have a tendency to behave negatively.
- ✔ Is facing left, you believe in tradition, are friendly, and remember dates including birthdays.
- ✔ Is facing forward (looking at you) you are direct, enjoy playing devil's advocate, and neither fear nor avoid discussions.
- ✔ Is facing right, you are innovative and active, but don't have a strong sense of family, nor do you remember dates.
- ✔ Was drawn with many details, you are analytical, cautious, and distrustful.
- ✔ Was drawn with few details, you are emotional and naive, care little for details, and are a risk-taker.
- ✔ Was drawn with four legs showing, you are secure, stubborn, and stick to your ideals.
- ✔ Was drawn with less than four legs showing, you are insecure, or are living through a period of major change.

Further, the size of the pig's ears indicate how good a listener the artist is—large is good. *(Adult groups only)* And the length of the pig's tail—again, more is better—indicates the quality of the artist's sex life.

27 Euclid's Triangle

Activity Type: Energizer

Group Size: Any number

Materials: Six straight, equal size objects (straws, pencils, match sticks, etc.) for each person or group

Time: 10 to 15 minutes

Procedure: Give each person or group the six objects. Instruct them to use the objects to form eight triangles. They are not allowed to bend or break the objects. The answer is shown above.

I would suggest that you start the activity by having individuals try to solve it on their own. After this is tried have them work in groups.

Processing Questions:

1. Was the objective clear from the instructions you received?
2. How was the solution different from your interpretation of the instructions?
3. Did it help to work in groups?

28 12 Squares

Activity Type: Energizer

Group Size: 10 to 30

Materials: Pencil and a piece of paper for each student

Time: 15 to 25 minutes

Procedure: Fold the paper in half, then fold it in half again. Then take the folded piece and fold it in thirds. When opened, the paper will have 12 spaces marked by the folds. The paper should look like this diagram:

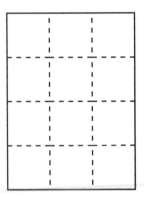

Have the group number the squares. Next, instruct the group to think of twelve questions that they could ask group members in order to find out information about them. Write these questions in the squares.

Examples: What is your favorite color? Food? Sports team? Music? Radio station?
What would you do if you won the lottery?

On the signal of "begin," the group will move around, interviewing each other and answering each other's questions which may be different or the same for each person. Students should write down the names of the persons they interviewed. Record their answers by their names.

Energizers—Calisthenics for the Mind

NOTE: When answering questions, individuals will only answer the same question once. Have them let the questioner know that they have already been asked that question.

After people have had a chance to interview twelve people, the group forms a circle and one by one share the responses they had on each person.

29 Memory Tricks

Activity Type: Energizer

Group Size: Any amount

Materials: Sheet of paper and pen or pencil for each student

Time: 20 to 30 minutes

Procedure: Have the students clear their desks and minds while you create a visual picture for them. Tell them that there will be 13 items in this picture. The picture goes as follows: On the floor there will be a stack including the following items:

1. A large **delicate plate**

2. A large **pen**

3. On top of the pen is a **Jersey calf**

4. Riding the calf is **King George**

5. On King George's face is a cut with a **bandage connecting the end of the cut**

6. On top of King George's head is a large **mass of ice**

7. On top of the ice is **Marilyn Maxwell**

8. Marilyn is holding a model of an **ocean liner headed south**

9. In the smoke stack of the model is a **ham**

10. The ham is wrapped in **sheet music** titled, "Carry Me Back to Old Virginia"

11. On top of the ham is a model of the **Empire State building**

---

12. On top of the model is a **weather vain** in the shape of an ocean liner headed north
13. On the weather vain is a **chicken**, a Rhode Island Red chicken

As you introduce each item make sure and repeat it at least three times and have class members say the list with you.

After you have gone through the list and the students understand it, ask them to take out their paper and write down the original 13 colonies. They will object and say they cannot do it. Show them that by using the list they are able to accomplish this task.

1. Delicate Plate......................................Delaware
2. Pen ....Pennsylvania
3. Jersey Calf......................................New Jersey
4. King George ....Georgia
5. Bandage Connecting...................Connecticut
6. Mass of ice...............................Massachusetts
7. Marilyn Maxwell .... Maryland
8. Ocean Liner Headed South... South Carolina
9. Ham..New Hampshire
10. Sheet Music ....Virginia
11. Empire State Building ....New York
12. Weather Vain ....North Carolina
13. Chicken......................................Rhode Island

Ask them to try to forget this information by the next day. On the next day retest them.

Processing Questions:

1. How does creating a visual picture help with learning?

2. Do they have any examples of similar activity in their learning?

3. How do advertisers and companies use these methods?

4. How can this relate to their school work?

30 Count Up

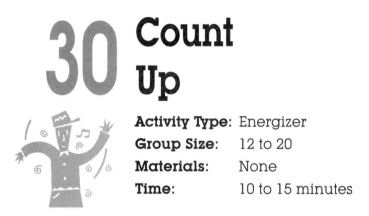

Activity Type: Energizer
Group Size: 12 to 20
Materials: None
Time: 10 to 15 minutes

Procedure: Have the group form a circle. Instruct them to begin milling around the room on your signal to start. Let them walk for 20 to 30 seconds and then tell them to stop and freeze on your command. When they freeze, the group should be facing many different directions. The task is to have the group count to 21 without anyone repeating a number or saying consecutive numbers. If they do, the group must start counting again from 0. (It may help to use a sheet of paper with 1 to 21 written on it and cross off the numbers as they are said.)

Processing Questions:

1. What were some of the frustrations you felt as you were doing this task?
2. Did a pattern develop in the process of the activity?
3. How does this activity relate to group tasks in daily life?

31 Photographic Memory

Activity Type: Energizer

Group Size: 12 to 18 (Can be divided into 2 groups)

Materials: None

Time: 20 minutes, or until everyone has a turn

Procedure: Choose three to four members of your group to be leaders. Their job is to stand up in front of the group and introduce themselves. After each person does this, have that person leave the room and change one thing about his or her physical appearance. Then the individual returns to the room and the group tries to guess what has been changed.

This can be a team competition by dividing the group in half with each side sending up different leaders. Give points to the team that guesses correctly.

NOTE: The changes that the leaders make should be visible, (i.e., moving shoes to the wrong foot, hair parted on opposite side, shirt inside out, etc.).

Processing Questions:

1. How hard was it to think of something to change?

2. Would the change have been noticed had we not been playing the game?

3. Do we spend too much time on aspects of personal appearance?

32 Comfort Zones

Activity Type: Energizer
Group Size: Any number
Materials: None
Time: Five minutes or less

Procedure: This activity is use to divide large groups into smaller groups. The goal is to get the participants out of their familiar surroundings and force them to encounter different people.

Decide ahead of time the number you would like in each group. Now let them form groups of that number, and have each group decide who in their group is north, south, east and west. Colors, numbers, animals, etc. can be used for smaller or larger groups. Then direct the participants into their new groups, (i.e., north, south, east, west).

The theory is most people when asked to get into a group will choose to be with friends (in their comfort zones). In the first step you allow them to do that.

In the second step you break them away from their initial group into new groups. Discuss the concept of comfort zones, and then do the activity that you have planned for the groups.

Processing Questions:

1. How did you choose the people that you grouped up with at first?

2. What was accomplished by having you regroup?

3. What are some reasons that we should work in groups with people other than our friends?

Carl Olson

33 Thinking Outside the Box

Activity Type: Energizer

Group Size: Two teams of 6 to 12 members

Materials: A display to write on: blackboard, flip chart, or overhead

Time: 10 to 15 minutes

Procedure: This is a good activity to start or end a class or group session. In this activity you give your group the first three clues of a sequence. Then ask them to try and figure out the next level. You can have them work individually or in groups. The sequence is as follows:

1

1 1

2 1

After they work on it for awhile, give them the next level. It is as follows:

1 2 1 1

Once again have the group make attempts to solve the problem. I use this as an assignment. After they solve it, I ask them to go home and try it on their family. The next day I have them report their experiences.

Solution: Level one is simply one. The next level will tell what was in the level before it. Example: Level two will have two ones because it tells us that the top level is one one (1, 1). Subsequently, level three tells us that the level above it has two ones (2, 1), and the next level is one two, and one one (1, 2, 1, 1). The extended sequence will be as follows:

1

1 1

2 1

1 2 1 1

1 1 1 2 2 1

3 1 2 2 1 1

1 3 1 1 2 2 2 1

1 1 1 3 2 1 3 2 1 1

Processing Questions:

1. Why is this activity named "Thinking outside the box?"

2. What would have been some good hints to help you solve the problem?

3. Please try this activity on someone else and report back how it worked.

Carl Olson

34 Squaring the Square

Activity Type: Energizer

Group Size: Any number

Materials: 12 straight, equal size objects (straws, pencils, match sticks, etc.) for each person or group

Time: 10 to 15 minutes

Procedure: Give each person or group the twelve objects, and have them arrange them as follows:

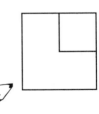

The task is for the individual or group to remove two objects to end up with two squares. The trick is solved by removing object A and B.

When A and B are removed, you'll have a square within a square as shown.

Processing Questions:

1. Was the solution different from the ideas you first thought about?

2. Try this on someone outside the group and report back with the results.

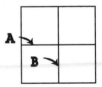

35 Seasons of the Year

Activity Type: Energizer
Group Size: Any number
Materials: None
Time: 15 Minutes

Procedure: Have the seasons of the year as the last change in the incorporation game. Divide into four groups by birthdays:

Group #1   Winter (December, January, February)

Group #2   Spring (March, April, May)

Group #3   Summer (June, July, August)

Group #4   Fall (September, October, November)

Have each group go to a different area of the room to compile a list of reasons why it is best to be born in their season. When their list is complete, they should present the reasons to the entire group.

Processing Questions:

No formal processing necessary. The object of the activity is to get your group to mix; doing the activity accomplishes this.

Carl Olson

36

Be a Star

Activity Type: Energizer

Group Size: Any number. It does work well for classroom size groups and smaller.

Materials: One "Be a Star" worksheet (#36A) for each student and nine objects (coins or bingo chips work well).

Time: 15 to 30 minutes, or until solution

Procedure: Instruct the students to follow the rules on the "Be A Star" worksheet. Demonstrate the correct method. It works well to make an overhead of the worksheet for this demonstration. (See the attached play sheet for instructions.)

In order to complete this activity correctly, you must always place your coin where the last coin started it's move. If you keep doing this pattern, you will be able to lay down all nine coins, and one space will be empty.

Processing Questions:

1. What were some of the feelings when you failed?

2. What clues helped you solve the problem?

3. Successful completion required knowing the pattern. What are some life areas that required learning patterns?

36A Be a Star

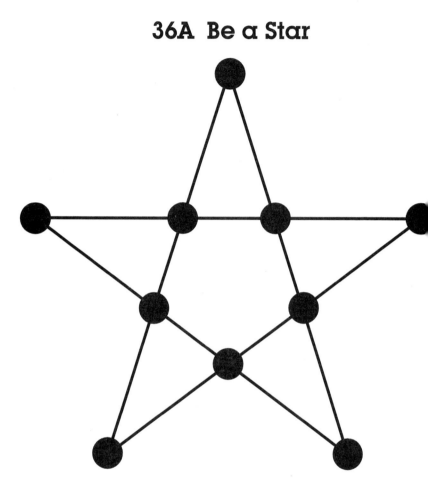

The object is to cover all but one of the dots with nine coins. In order to put a coin on a dot, you must move it like a checker piece over two dots in a straight line. Start your first coin on an unoccupied dot and jump over the next dot, placing your coin on the second dot in line.

A coin can move over an occupied dot, but can not land on an occupied dot. As you put down coins, the dots will fill up and make it difficult to lay down all nine coins.

Carl Olson

37 Nim

Activity Type: Energizer

Group Size: Any number

Materials: "Nim" worksheet (#37A) and 13 objects that can be laid on a desk or table. Toothpicks or paper clips work very well.

Time: 10 minutes

Procedure: Follow the directions on the attached sheet. When you follow the suggested procedures you will always win. Challenge the students to observe and then try to beat you. I always allow time to play after our regular work is done.

Processing Questions:

1. How does it feel to always lose at such a seemingly simple task?

2. What methods did you use to try and figure out the answer?

37A Nim

Direction Sheet

Set up 12 objects as follows:

X X X

X X X X

X X X X X

Rules:

1. Two people play the game.
2. Each person will takes turn removing objects from the set up.
3. When it is your turn, you may take as many objects as you want, but only from one row.
4. The person who has to take the last object is the looser.

Solution:

1. In order to win every time, you must go first and take two from the top row. See diagram below.

X

X X X X

X X X X X

2. In order to win, you have to get the same number in two rows and have it be the other person's turn. See diagram below:

X X X X

X X X X

3. The other way to win is to have a combination of 1-2-3 and have it be the other persons turn. See the diagram below:

X

X X

X X X

You can play the game often and you will win most of the time. This creates interest in the class or group.

38 Look Up Look Down

Activity Type: Energizer
Group Size: 6 to 24
Materials: None
Time: 10 minutes

Procedure: Have your group form a close circle that is shoulder to shoulder. All group members start by looking down at their feet. On your command, instruct them to look up and stare at one of the people in the circle. They are required to look at a different person each time. If the person they are looking at is also looking at them, they are both eliminated from the game. The eliminated people step back and the circle becomes smaller. Call out "look down" followed by "look up" and the process is repeated. Play is continued until there a winner or two people are left.

Variation: If you have a group where all the people know each other, you can play by the same rules, but allow one of the pair that look at each other to stay in the game by saying the other person's name as fast as possible. If they both say each other's name at the same time, they both would stay in the game. If they say someone's name that is not looking at them, they would be out.

Processing Questions:

1. What did it feel like to be eliminated from the game?
2. Did you follow the correct directions?
3. What did you do to try to use to stay in the game?

39 The Big Wind Blows

Activity Type: Energizer

Group Size: 10 to 40

Materials: One chair (without arms) per person

Time: 10 to 15 minutes

Procedure: Have all the participants make a circle with their chairs. Take away the chair of one person and have that person stand in the center of the circle. The person without a chair is "it." That person is instructed to say the following: "The big wind blows on people who...." At this point, the person can choose any characteristic that members of the group would have.

Example: People who have blonde hair

Are wearing shorts

Took a shower this morning

After the command is made, all the people who fall into the called category must get up and find a new seat. The "it" person also attempts to get a seat and the person who doesn't get a seat becomes "it" and the process starts over.

Processing Questions:

1. What did it feel like when you had to move?
2. Were you ever it in the game? If so how did you decide what category to choose?
3. Were you trying to win at the game?
4. Was it fun?
5. How does this relate to completive activities in your everyday life?

40 Add'em

Activity Type: Energizer

Group Size: Any Number

Materials: Overhead Projector, Add'em Overhead slide

Time: 5-10 minutes

Procedure: Make an overhead slide with the numbers in the box:

1,001
2,000
9
40
1,000
50

Start the activity with the slide covered. As you uncover the numbers one at a time, instruct the group to say the numbers in unison and add them together. Start by uncovering the first number and have them say it together (1,001). Cover it up and tell them they can do better! Repeat this process until they are energetically working together and adding in unison. Uncover the first number (1001); and the second number(2000); add them together(3001). Keep going until you have uncovered the entire column. At this time, about half of the group will give the correct total (4,100); half the group usually will say 5,000. Process what happened.

Processing Questions:

1. Why do some people make a mistake and say the total is 5,000? (following the group, mental error, didn't take time to think)

2. What other mistakes have you made doing activities that are relatively uncomplicated?

3. How can you be more careful and eliminate foolish mistakes?

Carl Olson

41 10 Nouns

Activity Type: Energizer

Group Size: 12 to 24

Materials: Writing supplies, markers, and newsprint

Time: 30 to 60 minutes

Procedure: Each person in the group should have paper and a pencil. Ask each member to think of ten nouns that would represent him or her. It is very important that the word be a noun and not an adjective. Have them write the nouns on their papers. (Examples: brother, athlete, rural, and so forth)

After this is completed, have them narrow their list down to five nouns, choosing the five they feel most strongly describe who they are. When they are finished, the group leader will have each person read their noun list to the group. As the individual lists are being read, the group leader will write the nouns on the newsprint pad.

The leader should then explain that the information on the sheet is not all that evident when you meet a person for the first time. It is, however, a part of each person's story and it is information that we need to know if we are to truly know and understand someone.

Processing Questions:

1. How many of the things on each list are visible when we meet someone for the first time?

2. What does this tell you about getting to know someone?

3. Would anyone have liked to changed or added to his or her list as they say what others put down?

Games

42 Musical Chairs

Activity Type: Game

Group Size: One chair (without arms) for each person CD or tape player and CD or tape of upbeat or lively music

Materials: "Birthday Surprise" (#7A) overhead

Time: 15 to 20 minutes

Procedure: Put the chairs into two lines, back-to-back. There should be one less chair than the number of people in the group. Play the music and have the group walk around the chairs. Stop the music and have all try to find a seat. The person without a chair is the loser, but instead of eliminating that person from the game, have the individual remain sitting in one of the chairs. This gives the group still playing the game one less chair from which to choose. Continue playing as long as you like. I usually go until there are 4 to 5 chairs left and then start over.

This way of playing musical chairs allows eliminated players a means of staying active in the game. They still feel involved and the group has greater enjoyment.

Processing Questions:

1. What were we trying to accomplish by playing the game?

2. How is this game of musical chairs different from others you have played?

3. How can we relate these differences to what we are trying to accomplish in our group setting?

43 Catastrophe

Activity Type: Game

Group Size: 30 to 75 (In our school we choose 25 students from each grade 6 to 8)

Materials: One chair for each participant. An occupation marker for each participant. Labels or buttons work well. I use buttons as they can be used from year-to-year. (Worksheet #43A)

Time: 15 to 20 minutes

Procedure: (See attached sheet #43A for rules.)

NOTE: Safety is a number one concern. To help with this I bring in each team for training. With twenty-five students, I try to call one from each group of five at each set. This keeps them spaced.

Processing Questions:

1. What was it like to be on the class team?
2. Was it difficult to stay focused under pressure?
3. What was it like to win? To lose?

43A Catastrophe

This is a game that can be done at an assembly and can involve many students. I use it as a competition between the 6th, 7th, and 8th grade students in my school. Students are eligible to play through a drawing and all other students watch the game and cheer for their grade.

The model involves 45 students, each assigned an occupation and a chair. The chairs are set up in straight lines, one line per grade. The lines of chairs are referred to as streets. You can add or subtract students by adding or subtracting occupations. I even make badges for the students in the game indicating their specific occupations.

The object of the game is for different occupations to respond to "emergencies." This simply means that if a student's assigned occupation is called, that student is to run all the way around the group (or street) and back to the assigned seat. To keep students spaced while playing the game, I usually call one student from each group of five at each turn. For example, the police officer, nurse, astronaut, and actor would be called at the same time. The first class to get all the called occupations back to their seats wins the turn and receives one point. There is a representative teacher placed at the front of each grade street to judge the competition. As soon as the occupations of a specific grade are back in their seats, the teacher raises his or her hand. The leader will watch for the first hand raised. If the leader calls out, "CATASTROPHE," all the occupations must run around their specific street and return to their seats. The winner is the first team to reach ten points.

Carl Olson

Set up the gym as follows: _____ indicates chairs and the chairs face the crowd

CROWD

LEADER (in a position so that you can see the crowd and the game)

	JUDGE (facing line) 6TH STREET	JUDGE (facing line) 7TH STREET	JUDGE (facing line) 8TH STREET
Police Officer	_____	_____	_____
Doctor	_____	_____	_____
Lawyer	_____	_____	_____
Fire Fighter	_____	_____	_____
Nurse	_____	_____	_____
Garbage Collector	_____	_____	_____
Dentist	_____	_____	_____
Baker	_____	_____	_____
Painter	_____	_____	_____
Astronaut	_____	_____	_____
Teacher	_____	_____	_____
Cook	_____	_____	_____
Farmer	_____	_____	_____
Musician	_____	_____	_____
Actor	_____	_____	_____

Procedure:

1. The leader calls out, "There is an emergency on sixth or eighth street and the following occupation(s) are needed...." As the leader, you need to decide on each turn if the emergency is on sixth or eighth street. This is said so that the students know which way to turn and run around the group. When the leader says that the emergency is on sixth street, all the students playing the game should shift in their chairs and face the left side of the room. If the leader says that the emergency is on eighth street, all the students should face the right side of the room.

2. The students of the called occupation(s) go to the left or right according to what street was called and they run around their entire street and back to their seats. Students should run towards the back of their group first and then around the front.

3. If the leader calls "CATASTROPHE," all students on all streets should run around their groups and back to their seats. It is very important to indicate which street an emergency is on before calling it a catastrophe. For example, "There is an emergency on sixth street (students should face to the left) and it is a catastrophe!"

4. One point goes to the team whose members get back to their seats first. (Be sure they have exited from the correct side.) Again, the winner is the first team to reach ten points.

NOTE: Safety is a number one concern in this game, so I bring in each team for training prior to the actual game.

44 Zoom Erk

Activity Type: Game

Group Size: 8 to 30

Materials: None

Time: 10 to 20 minutes (can be repeated)

Procedure: Have the group sit in a circle. The game requires that we move around the circle without making a mistake. The message is the sound of a car—zoom. The person who starts looks in the direction he or she wants to go and says: "Zoom." The person he or she is looking at continues without hesitation. If anyone hesitates, that person is out of the game. That person moves the chair back and the game continues.

If the message receiver wants to change the direction, it can be done in two ways:

1. To reverse directions, the receiver would say "Erk." At this point the message is going the other direction. *NOTE:* Erk cannot be followed by Erk.

2. To go across the circle you say the person's name you want to pick up the message. Example: "Zoom, John." John would have to keep the message going.

You keep playing until there are 5 or 6 players left. Players who have been eliminated should act as judges.

Processing Questions:

1. What is the object of the game?
2. What is it like to play under pressure?
3. What are some areas of life that we work under similar pressures?
4. What can we do to increase our performance and thought process in pressure situations?

45 Electricity

Activity Type: Game

Group Size: 18 to 30

Materials: One ball or soft object to grab

Time: 15 to 25 minutes

Procedure: Divide the class into two teams. Have them sit back-to-back in two even lines.

X X X X X X X X X X

Leader **O**   **o** Object

X X X X X X X X X X

NOTE: The first two and last two people face in and the rest of the team faces out.

The people in each line hold hands and the only people who are allowed to have their eyes open are the first two. The leader flips a coin and shows the first two people. If heads comes up, they squeeze the person's hand next to them and the squeeze is passed down the line. When the squeeze (message) reaches the last person, they try to grab the object before the other team gets it.

Score one point for each successful message. If they send a wrong message (they don't squeeze on tails), one point is subtracted. Rotate the lines so all the players get to position #1.

Processing Questions:

1. When did you feel the most involved or under pressure?
2. Did your team send a wrong message?
3. How can we compare a wrong message to rumors?

---

46 **Buzz**

Activity Type: Game
Group Size: 8 to 30
Materials: None
Time: 10 to 15 minutes

Procedure: Arrange the group in a circle. Count to fifty, moving around the circle. The count must move around the circle without hesitation. The special rules for the count are as follows:

1. The count will continue until they get to a number with a 7 in it. (7, 17, 27, 37, 47, etc.) At this point, instead of saying the number with a 7 in it, the person would say "Buzz" and the count would reverse directions.

2. In addition to numbers that have 7 in them, they will also "Buzz" on numbers that are multiples of 7. (7, 14, 21, 28, etc.) Challenge the group to see how high they can get. Always start the count at a different point in the circle.

Processing Questions:

1. Were there any problems understanding the rules?

2. Why is an activity that seems to be so easy end up being hard?

3. What was the mood of the group as we did this activity?

4. What did it feel like to make a mistake?

Carl Olson

47 Balloon Train

Activity Type: Game

Group Size: Any number

Materials: One balloon for each person

Time: 5 to 10 minutes

Procedure: Split the group into teams with even numbers on each team. This is a relay race type event. Have a starting line and a cone or chair that the team needs to move around and go back. Members will blow up balloons and they will be used as spacers between themselves and the person in front of them. On the "go" command, the whole team moves ahead, keeping the balloons between themselves without using their hands. If a balloon drops, the whole train must stop, reposition, and then continue.

Processing Questions:

1, What were some of the difficulties in playing this game successfully?

2. Was it better to try and go fast or slow?

3. How did you know if your teammates behind you were having trouble?

4. Are there group tasks you are faced with that require this same type thinking?

---

48 Train Wreck

Activity Type: Game

Group Size: 10 to 30

Materials: One chair (without arms) per participant

Time: 15 to 20 minutes

Procedure: Line the chairs up in two rows facing the same direction (see diagram). Have the students take chairs. Give all students a number from one through the number of participants. One of the students is picked to be the conductor. Set up a scenario where all the students are on a moving train.

They will be allowed to get up and move when their number is called. They may only move down the aisle of the train—the center space between the two rows.

xxxxxxxxxxxxxxxx

Aisle

xxxxxxxxxxxxxxxx

All chairs face this direction

The conductor walks up and down the aisle and, when ready, calls out numbers, (i.e., 3, 6, 9, 12). At the conductor's command, the people who have the called number must find a new seat. The conductor also attempts to take an empty seat. After the exchange of seats, the person who does not have a seat is then the conductor.

If the conductor calls: "Train wreck," all people have to move.

NOTE: Number callers can get creative, (i.e., even numbers, number that end in "e," the square root of 9, multiples of "5," etc.).

Processing Questions:

1. In this game your sense of security requires that you have a chair. What feelings did you have when your number was called?

2. How did it feel not to have your number called?

3. Are there similar situations in daily lives?

49 Four on a Couch

Activity Type: Game

Group Size: 15 to 30 who know each other

Materials: Name cards, team markers, chairs (one per student)

See worksheet #49A.

Time: 25 to 30 minutes

Procedure: Split your group into teams. Mark the teams with different colored post-it notes. See worksheet #49A for a diagram, instructions, and rules.

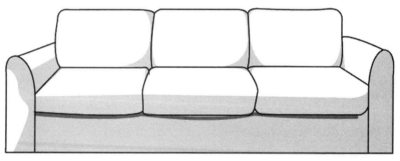

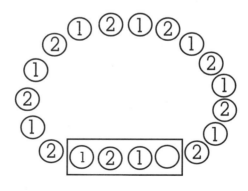

49A Four on a Couch

1. Divide the group into two equal teams. Indicate teams with colored post-its. Team members sit every other seat.

2. Have the students write their names on a card.

3. Collect and shuffle the cards and pass them out. It's okay if they get their own cards.

4. The room is set up with chairs in a semicircle facing four chairs in the front of the room.

5. Choose two players from one team and one from the other to sit on the couch. The one player should be seated between the other two.

6. The game is started by the player to the left of the empty couch seat. That person calls out any name. The person holding that card moves to the empty seat and the player who called the name and the player who moved exchange cards.

7. The next person to call will be the player to the left of the empty seat.

   NOTE:

   a, You cannot call the player who was just called.

   b. You cannot call the name of the card you are holding.

8. The first team to get four of their team members on the couch wins the game.

50 Elbow Tag

Activity Type: Game
Group Size: 12 to 30
Materials: None
Time: 15 to 20 minutes

Procedure: Have your group pair up and make a circle with partners standing next to each other and linking elbows. Pick two people to play the game. One person will be "it" and be required to chase the other person. If the "it" person tags the person he or she is chasing, that person becomes "it" and the rules are reversed.

The chased person can become safe by linking elbows with the end person of any of the pairs. By doing this, the person on the opposite end of the pair becomes the chased person.

The chased person must travel outside the circle. The person who is "it" may go through or around the circle.

Processing Questions:

1. In this game we passed responsibility from one person to another. Are there similar situations in our daily lives?
2. What did it feel like to be it?
3. The game combined competition and fun. Can we apply this to our group activities?

51 Gotcha

Activity Type: Game

Group Size: Any number—works best when you have more than 10.

Materials: "Gotcha" (#51A) worksheet, pencil, tickets

Time: 15 to 20 minutes

Procedure: Hand out pencils and "Gotcha" worksheets to all. Instruct the group that they will have 12 minutes to complete the items on the "Gotcha" worksheet. As they complete each task they must have the person sign who helped complete it.

Have numbered tickets available for people who finish ahead of time. Stress that you will have a drawing for fabulous prizes for all people who finish early.

For prizes you can give candy or nothing if you choose. I find that suggesting some reward heightens interest in most groups. I also find it effective to announce the time remaining. I also try to circulate to assist students who are having difficulty mixing and getting involved.

This activity works the best with new groups who do not know each other.

Processing Questions:

1. Why is it hard to interact with new groups of people?

2. Did you act different than you might have in a new situation? Why?

3. How many people were inspired by the chance of prizes?

4. Did everyone meet new people?

51A Gotcha!

Do everything listed here and get signatures to prove it. No duplicate signatures please!

1. Untie someone's shoe, then tie it again. Have the person sign here: _____

2. Count out loud (as loud as you can) as you do 10 jumping jacks with a partner. Partner sign here: _____

3. Find someone who is left-handed. Have that person write his or her name using the RIGHT hand here: _____
   _____

4. Have someone do 5 push-ups for you and sign his or her name here: _____

5. Get someone to sing a TV commercial and sign here: _____

6. Do your very BEST impersonation of a cow, pig, or chicken for someone and have that person sign here: _____

7. Find someone whose birthday is the same month as yours and sign name and month here: _____ & _____

8. Get 6 different autographs and their places of birth on the **back of this sheet.**

9. Find someone whose eyes are a different color from yours and sign here: _____
   _____

10. Get FOUR other people and you; form a circle and sing one verse of **ROW, ROW, ROW YOUR BOAT** and have them all sign on the **back of this sheet**.

11. Get a penny from someone and have that person sign here: _____

12. Find SIX people and have a group hug!

52 Zapper

Activity Type: Game
Group Size: Any number
Materials: None
Time: 15 to 20 Minutes

Procedure: Have the group sit in the activity area. All participants sit on the floor, put their heads down, and close their eyes! The facilitator walks among the group and touches one of the players on the head while walking by. After a short time, all participants are instructed to open their eyes and stand up. To play the game they must move around the room shaking hands with everyone in the group. The person who's head was touched is the Zapper. When the Zapper shakes hands, he or she can zap people by scratching their palms as they shake hands.

If your hand is scratched, you must count to 15 (in silence) and then act as though you were zapped by lightning, drop to the floor and stay there until the game is over. When a person is zapped, that person should use his or her best acting skills.

Play continues and, at anytime, a player who has not been zapped can stop the game and make an accusation naming the Zapper. If the accusation is correct, the game is over. If wrong, the accuser must also act like he or she was zapped.

Processing Questions:

1. What was it like to have the power to zap people?

2. Was it difficult to act out being zapped?

3. Could you sense any information from people even though you were not allowed to talk?

53 Blind Tic Tac Toe

Activity Type: Game

Group Size: Two teams of 4 to 16 players

Materials: Overhead transparency marked as follows:

Time: 15 to 20 minutes depending on the number of games

Procedure: The two teams will be the Xs and Os. There will be four members of each team playing at one time. They will be set up as follows:

Overhead Projector Screen

↓ x x x x o o o o ↓

(Facing away from the screen)

Choose a team to start and have one player at a time tell you where to place your mark. Teams alternate until one team wins or a cats game (tie) is declared. The starting team is alternated each game.

Processing Questions:

1. What problems did you encounter by not being able to see the game board?
2. Do we all see and explain things the same way?
3. Would have helped if we could ask questions or conferred?

54 Tic Tac Toe Race

Activity Type: Game

Group Size: Two teams of 6 to 12 members

Materials: Nine chairs set up as follows:

X X X

X X X

X X X

Time: 15 to 20 Minutes

Procedure: One team will be the X team and the other O. Have the two teams number their members with consecutive numbers. If one team has one more player, the team with less will designate one player to have two numbers. The teams should line up in front of the chairs.

Team X   **Team O**

X X X

X X X

X X X

The game is played by having the facilitator call out three random numbers. The people with those numbers will run to the chairs and try to form a Tic Tac Toe (3 players in a row either vertically, horizontally or diagonally). The X players cross their arms above their head and the O team forms an O with their arms. The players keep moving around until they win. The process is repeated as often as you choose.

55 Name That Tune

Activity Type: Game

Group Size: 2 to 6 groups of 6-12 players

Materials: A cassette tape and player, and pencil and paper for each group. The tape should have short parts of various songs with many different types of music. I recommend 12 to 15 songs.

Time: Varies according to the length of time it takes to divide into groups, play the tape, and score the contest.

Procedures: Divide your group into equal subgroups. Each group will pick a recorder. The recorder will have a pencil and sheet of paper.

Play the tape and have each group try to name the tunes with the recorder writing the answer on the paper. Give an additional point if the group can name the artist.

56 Two Truths and a Lie

Activity Type: Game

Group Size: 6 to 18

Materials: None

Time: Enough time for each to participate

Procedure: Have the individual participants think of three interesting things about themselves. Two of the three would be true and one false. For example, my description would be:

1. I was related to the Lone Ranger.
2. My son is a professional golfer.
3. I have a dog named Joey.

The group then has to decide which of the three statements is false. After all group members give their opinions, each member reveals which two are true. (In this case my wife's uncle was the Lone Ranger, my son is a professional golfer, but I don't have a dog named Joey.)

This is a great way to have a group become more familiar with each other plus it makes it so much easier for them to start conversations and develop friendships.

Processing Questions:

1. Did you learn something about the other people in the group?
2. Was it hard to think of the three things about yourself?
3. What was it like trying to sell the untruth about yourself?
4. What can we do to continue to get to know more about each other?

57 Who Am I?

Activity Type: Game

Group Size: Any Number

Materials: Name cards and pins for each group member

Time: 20 to 30 minutes

Procedure: Think up various names of famous people—they can be alive, dead or fictitious. Assign a famous person to each member of your group. Put the card with the famous person's name on it on the back of the assigned person. Do not allow the rest of the group see the name on his or her card.

After all the group has their cards on their backs, they are free to go around and ask fellow group members questions about who they are. All questions should be answered only with yes and no answers. A good basic rule is to only allow two questions from each person. This will result in more group interaction.

Processing Questions:

1. Did you follow the rules at all times?
2. How many different people did you ask questions of?
3. Does your famous person have anything in common with you?
4. Did you meet any new people?

58 Blanket Drop

Activity Type: Game

Group Size: 12 to 20 divided into two equal teams

Materials: A blanket or piece of dark plastic

Time: 10 to 20 minutes

Procedure: Divide the group into two equal teams. Have two people hold up a blanket as a divider. Have the groups sit on opposite sides of the room facing the divider. The two sides cannot see each other as shown below:

```
XXXXXX | XXXXXX
XXXXXX | XXXXXX
```

Divider

The people holding the blanket drop it quickly. When the blanket is dropped the two people at the front of the line try to say the name of the person facing them. The person that says the correct name first wins. The loosing person then goes over to the other team.

When the blanket is raised, different people move to the front of the line. The game continues. The winning team will have the largest number of members.

This activity is a great energizer. It is also a means of having groups get to know each others names.

Initiatives

59 One-Way/ Two-Way Communication

Activity Type: Initiative

Group Size: Any number works well with a classroom group. Students will pair up with a partner.

Materials: In each activity, the person whose back is to the overhead has a blank piece of paper and a pencil to follow the instructions. The instructor will need the activity overheads 59A and 59B.

The instructor will need the activity overheads 59A and 59B.

Time: 15 to 20 minutes

Procedure: Have the group pair up and sit so that one partner is facing the overhead screen and the other is facing away (back-to-back). The person facing away is the drawer and the other person describes the drawing. In phase one of one-way communication, the drawing is explained as the only form of communication. No questions are allowed and the person explaining cannot look at what is being drawn.

In phase two, I have the people switch places and use drawing #2. This is a two way process, as the person drawing may ask questions. After finishing, the two experiences are compared. I find that it it's best to use this in combination with Activity #60, Broken Squares. The activity Broken Squares uses no communication, and in phase one we move to a level of one way communication and in phase two to a level of two way communication. This activity allows us to compare these levels of communication.

Processing Questions:

1. What were the disadvantages of the level one activity?
2. Why do we call this one way communication?
3. Where is this used in everyday life?
4. How was level II better?
5. How could this process become even better?

59A One-Way Communication

Drawing #1

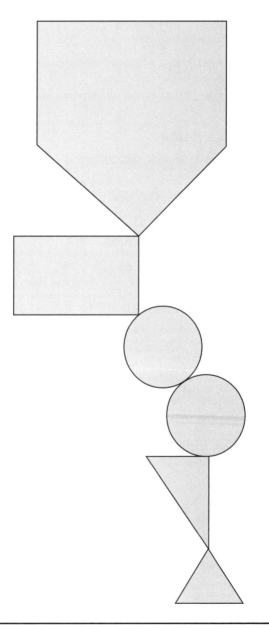

Carl Olson

57B Two-Way Communication

Drawing #2

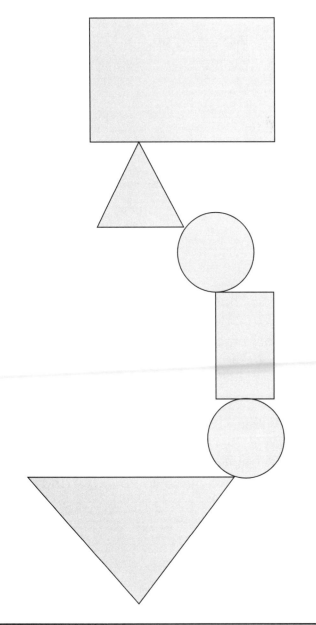

60 Broken Squares

Activity Type: Initiative

Group Size: See #60A. Small group to classroom size will work. Sub-groups of five need to be formed. Have any extra students act as monitors. Sit at a table or on the floor.

Materials: Five envelopes per group with parts of the broken squares in them. Arranged as explained in the set up.

Time: 20 to 30 minutes with processing

Procedure: Break the group into five person sub-groups. Give the instructions. (See #60A for square patterns and instructions.)

Processing Questions:

1. What was it like not being able to communicate?
2. Did you see a solution for someone else and could not help them?
3. Did you see a piece you needed and could not ask for it?
4. Did anyone in your group make a wrong square?
5. Was anyone under pressure because they were stuck but other people knew what to do?
6. How could we improve this process?

60A Broken Squares

The Set-Up

Five pieces of stiff paper (cut into 6" squares) make one set.

1. Cut and label the squares according to the diagram below:

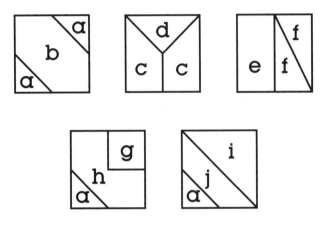

2. Place the pieces in five envelopes. There should be 3 pieces in each envelope. The pieces should be mixed up so that no envelope contains the correct combination of parts to make a square.

   NOTE: Several combinations of the pieces will form one or two squares, but only one combination will form five squares.

3. Divide the students into five groups of five.

4. Pass out one envelope per group.

Game Rules:

Instruct the players that there are exactly enough parts distributed among the five people to make five complete squares. Their task is completed when a square is put together in front of each person in each group.

1. Players may not talk, signal, or gesture in any way that would provide guidance or direction to another group member.
2. Players may give any of their pieces of the puzzle to another player in their group.
3. Each player's puzzle pieces must be in front of the player, except when passing a piece to another player.

Discussion:

1. How did you feel during the activity?
2. How did your group function? Was there a pattern?
3. Did you follow the rules?
4. Did a leader identify himself or herself?
5. How did your group define cooperation?

61 If Eggs Could Fly

Activity Type: Initiative

Group Size: 4 to 5 per small group

Materials: 1 egg, 1 paper bag, 1 balloon, 3 feet of masking tape, a paper clip, 4 cotton balls, 20 straws

Time: 30 to 40 minutes

Procedure: Do a warm-up activity, (i.e., Look Up, Look Down) and then split the group into subgroups of 4 to 5. Give each group the materials list and have them spend 8 to 10 minutes planning a vehicle to provide safe environment for their egg when dropped from ten feet.

After the planning phase, give them 10 to 12 minutes for the actual construction of their vehicle. Next test the vehicle by dropping it from 10 feet. *NOTE:* The floor should be covered with plastic. Test all the vehicles, then process the activity.

Processing Questions:

1. How many different ideas did you consider during planning?

2. Did all group members have a say in what was decided?

3. What roles did each person play in your group?

62 The Magic Dot

Activity Type: Initiative

Group Size: 5 to 30

Materials: Tape, 3 colored dots per group

Time: 20 to 30 minutes

Procedure: Divide the group into subgroups of five students. With each group of five, have them choose a person to act as the jumper. The other members of the group will act as observers. Put a taped line on the floor. The jumper takes one try to make a standing long jump. Mark the distance with a blue dot. After the first jump, have the observers give feedback to the jumper regarding ways he or she can improve.

After the feedback session, a second jump is taken. This jump is marked with a different colored dot. In most cases this second attempt will show improvement.

A final attempt is set up. This time the observers are asked to give encouragement (cheering, etc.). Before this final attempt the groups and the jumper set a goal by putting a different color of dot one inch beyond the longest effort so far. The final attempt is then completed. In most cases the jumper will meet or exceed that goal.

         Carl Olson

Processing Questions:

1. What was it like to be the jumper?
2. What was it like to be an observer?
3. How did the second phase help the jumpers?
4. What are some reasons that the second attempt improved?
5. Did observers feel that they made a contribution?
6. What was the value of goal setting with the orange dot?

63 Reverse Pyramid

Activity Type: Initiative

Group Size: 10 people form the pyramid; extra people can act as observers/problem solvers

Materials: None

Time: 10 to 15 minutes

Procedure: Have your 10 people line up in a pyramid formation. When done they will all be facing the same direction with rows of 1, 2, 3, and 4. See the diagram. Challenge the group to reverse the direction of the pyramid by only moving three people. The answer is shown in diagram.

FORMATION   **SOLUTION**

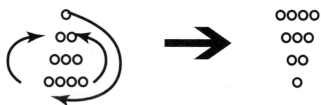

Be available to answer questions, but let them work out the problem.

Processing Questions:

1. How did your process develop?

2. Did anyone person take over the leadership role?

3. What were some frustrations with the process?

     Carl Olson

64 Random Numbers

Activity Type: Initiative

Group Size: 10 to 20

Materials: Spot numbers, boundary rope, starting line, timing watch

Time: 20 to 30 minutes

Procedure: Create a boundary area that is at least 15 feet square. Randomly put out 36 spot numbers in the boundary area. Have a starting line that is 20 to 30 feet from the boundary.

Have the group meet at the starting line and walk them through the process of the activity. Give the following rules:

1. The group's goal is to step on all of the numbers from 1 to 36 in order in the fastest time. There is no limit to the amount of numbers upon which one individual may step.

2. Only one team member is allowed in the boundary area at a time. Each violation of this rule adds 5 seconds to the group time.

3. The group will be given 5 minutes to plan how they will reach the goal.

4. The group will begin at the start line and move to the boundary area at the "go" command.

5. When all the numbers have been stepped on, the group must run back to the start line.

6. The group will be given a total of three trials with 5 minutes of planning and processing time between each one.

```
1    2  25   9       24
  26  14    4    16 27
  15  32   3    5   10  28
          19
  30  18  29   8   23  35
  33     7  12  31  11  6
  21              20  17
     22     13  34  36
```

Start Line

NOTE: Rubber spots can be purchased from sporting goods dealers or they can be made out of tile. Any rope can serve as the boundary area.

Processing Questions:

1. How did your trials differ from each other?
2. Did anyone emerge as a leader as you planned?
3. Did penalties detract from your performance?
4. Did you all agree on how best to do this activity?
5. What would you do differently if you had another try?

65 Inclusion/ Exclusion

Activity Type: Initiative
Group Size: 15 to 20
Materials: None
Time: 15 to 20 minutes

Procedure: Divide the group into three equal sub groups. Pick one person from each sub group. Have the three chosen people leave the room. This activity will be conducted in three phases.

Phase 1: Have the sub group form a tight circle, either sitting in chairs or standing with their arms around each other. Invite the three outside people back into the room and tell them to join their groups. In this phase the groups will ignore them, and not let them in the circles. Have this process go on for 2 to 3 minutes. Then send the three out of the room again. *(Each time the outsiders come back into the room they should go to a different circle.)*

Phase 2: This time the groups will let the outsiders in the circle, but they will ignore them and not include them in their conversations. Once again let the activity go for 2-3 minutes.

Phase 3: The outsiders are invited in this last time and the circle will accept them, include them in their conversation, and make them feel welcome.

Processing Questions:

Ask these questions after each role-play.

Phase 1

1. How does this happen in real life? Where do you see it happen?

2. How many of you have ever felt excluded from a group? (Raise hands)

3. What feelings do you remember having when you were excluded? How might it affect someone if they have several experiences of being excluded?

Phase 2

1. How does this role-play different from the first one?

2. Ask the "outsider": Did you like this role-play better or worse than the last one? Why?

3. Do people in real life just pretend to accept someone?

4. How do you feel about someone being treated this way?

Phase 3

1. Ask the "outsider": How was that?

66 A Man Bought a Horse

Activity Type: Initiative

Group Size: Any number—works well with classroom size

Materials: "A Man Bought a Horse" overhead worksheet (#66A)

Time: 10 to 20 minutes

Procedure: The directions can be found on the sheet mentioned above.

Processing Questions:

1. Why was it hard for everyone to come up with the same answer to this simple problem?

2. Did it help to share understanding with other students?

3. How can this process help out in other areas of life?

66A A Man Bought a Horse

Directions:

1. Solve the problem individually. Record your answer in the space provided below.

2. You will then be placed in a group of 2 to 4 people, and will then try to reach a consensus on the right answer to the problem below. Record the group answer in the space provided below.

The Problem:

A man bought a horse for sixty dollars and sold it for seventy dollars. He then bought the same horse back again for eighty dollars and sold it for ninety dollars. How much money did the man make in the horse trading business?

Individual Answer: _____

Group Answer: _____

Carl Olson

67 Northwoods Survival

Activity Type: Initiative

Group Size: Any number—grouped in smaller sub groups of 4 to 6

Materials: "Northwoods Survival" worksheet (#67A)

See worksheet #67B for the answers.

Time: 20 to 30 minutes

Procedure: *NOTE:* There are many of these types of activities that have been developed. I have found this one to work the best for me. I will include a list and samples of others in this section. Subdivide your larger group into smaller group of 4 to 6. Pass out the Northwoods Survival worksheet and read it out loud.

Ask them to pick out the top seven (they don't have to rank them) things a person would need for the trip back to the air base.

After they have done it individually, have them share their results in their group and come up with a list of seven that their group can agree on.

NOTE: I have done this for years and I have yet to have a group come up with the correct answers.

The next step would be a report from each group on their results. Follow this with processing.

Processing Questions:

1. What problems did you find when you did this on your own?
2. Did all group members come up with the same answers?
3. How did you decide which answers to use?
4. Did anyone suggest correct answers that you did not choose?
5. Did all members of your group contribute?
6. Where are some places that we need to use group agreement in everyday life?

67A Northwoods Survival Lab

You and your partner have planned
a week-long fly-in fishing trip in the
northern Ontario bush country.
About 40 miles from the air base,
the plane is forced down on a lake
that is too small for a safe landing.
The pilot lands, but is unable to stop
the plane before it plows into the
shoreline.

Your partner suffered a broken arm
and minor injuries, but he is able to
move around. The pilot is badly hurt and requires
immediate medical attention. The plane's radio is
destroyed. You are the only person in the party who
is not injured.

The terrain between you and the air base consists
of lakes, muskeg swamp, bogs, and virtually im-
penetrable woods. Counting the necessary detours
around these hazards, you estimate a trip of 80 to
100 miles to get out.

You must check the list of supplies and rank them
in order of importance for your survival on the trip
back to the air base. Place the number 1 next to
the most important item, 2 for the next most important, and so on.

____ 1 camp saw	____ 1 hatchet
____ lantern	____ camp stove
____ insect repellent	____ 2 first aid kits
____ 1 frypan	____ silverware
____ hand gun (.32 caliber)	____ map
____ 2 packs dried beef	____ fishing tackle
____ 1 pack dried apricots	____ compass
____ buoyant boat seat cushions	

67B Northwoods Survival Lab Answers

Priorities...

1. **COMPASS:** An absolute necessity — the woods are so thick in some places that ten steps can alter your direction 90°.

2. **MAP:** In order to select the best route around lakes and across rivers, the map could save hours of walking.

3. **INSECT REPELLENT:** The black flies and the mosquitoes in the bush country are thick and hungry. If you have never entered bush country, you can't imagine how thick.

4. **BOAT SEAT CUSHION:** The cushion is buoyant and would save miles of walking by allowing you to swim small lakes and rivers.

5. **DRIED BEEF**

6. **DRIED APRICOTS**

7. **ONE FIRST AID KIT:** In case of injury the survivors would need the other kit.

Low priority items...

8. **CAMP SAW:** Unnecessary because there is abundant firewood lying all over.

9. **HATCHET:** Unnecessary for the same reason.

10. **FISHING TACKLE:** You have enough food.

11. **LANTERN:** Impossible to travel at night.

12. **FRY PAN:** No food preparation necessary for dried food.

13. **CAMP STOVE:** No food preparation necessary for dried food.

14. **SILVERWARE:** Will not need for dried food.

15. **HANDGUN:** Little need for protection—only one chance in a thousand of meeting a bear.

68 Headbands

Activity Type: Initiative

Group Size: Any number

Materials: Headbands constructed as per attached handout (#68A) and masking tape

Time: 20 to 30 minutes

Procedure: Choose the number of volunteers as you have headband roles for. Seat the volunteers in front of your group so the volunteers can see each other and the members of the audience can see them. Set up a scenario where this group of volunteers is going to plan a special activity. A good example would be a dance or party. Something they would all have an opinion on.

Put on the headbands and instruct the group to treat each person as the headband calls for. Have the activity continue until all the volunteers get a feel for their roles.

Follow the activity with process.

Processing Questions:

1. Ask the volunteers what they might think their roles might be?
2. How could they sense it and how did it feel to play that role?
3. Do we treat people in some of these ways? Where? Why?
4. Which roles would be the easiest to play?
5. How can we make our groups more productive by the way we respect and treat people?

68A Headbands

PURPOSE: To demonstrate the invisible "role headbands" we place on people and how those perceptions influence how we treat others and how they respond to their roles.

ACTION: Six members form a panel, facing the rest of the group. On each head, place a headband, indicating their role in the group. The six do not know what their individual headbands say, but must be able to see the other headbands. The audience sees all headbands. The six are told that they area student council committee in charge of deciding and planning a major fund-raiser to raise money for a school service project.

They are raising money for a classmate who was injured and paralyzed in a car accident. The family needs money to make their home and vehicle handicap accessible, as well as for medical expenses.

The six are to treat each other as the headbands say. The audience is to observe. The roles are:

1. Always ask for my opinion.
2. Agree with everything I say.
3. Make fun of everything I say.
4. Ignore me.
5. Disagree with everything I say.
6. I'm intelligent.

Processing Questions:

1. Ask the panelists to guess their roles.

2. How did they know? How did they feel when others treated them that way?

3. Discuss how we label people. Ask for examples.

4. What are the problems caused by labels? Or by cliques?

5. Why might someone choose a certain role, such as a class clown?

6. Are roles always true or do they mask reality?

69 Who Has the Answer?

Activity Type: Initiative

Group Size: Any number

Materials: "Who Has the Answer?" (#69A) overhead worksheet

Time: 15 to 25 minutes

Procedure: Hand out "Who Has the Answer?" worksheet or display on the overhead. Ask the group to try to select the one shape that is different from **all** the others. Have them work individually at first, then put them in small groups. This process should take 5 minutes.

Have several groups tell what they got for an answer and why. After you complete this part of the process, finish the exercise by pointing out that none of the figures is different from all the rest.

Processing Questions:

1. How did you come up with your first answer and why?
2. Did you have any doubts or concerns about original answer?
3. Did you have the same answer as the people you were grouped with?
4. Did anyone change their mind?
5. Do we have problems in real life that do not have clear cut answers?

69A Who Has the Answer?

Exercise: Five figures are shown below. Select the one that is different from all of the others.

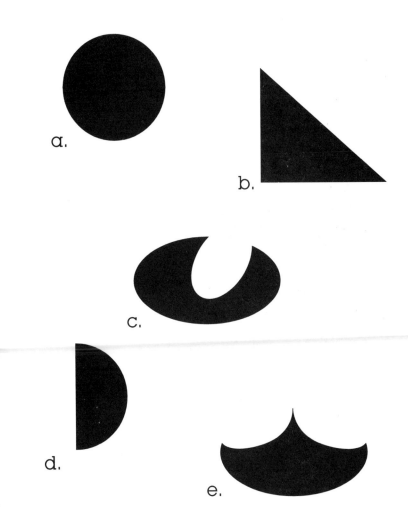

a.

b.

c.

d.

e.

70 Checkerboard Challenge

Activity Type Initiative

Group Size: 6 to 24

Materials: Instructions for game (see #70A) and some means of laying out a checkerboard.

Time: 15 to 30 minutes

Procedure: Have the group stand at one end of the checkerboard. See the attached drawing and give instructions.

1. Each person takes a turn choosing a step.
2. If the step is correct, I will say "yes" or "okay," if wrong, I will say "no."
3. Steps can be forward, sideways, or diagonal—not backwards.
4. Indicate the number of steps needed to complete the exercise.
5. The entire group must make it through the maze in order to complete the activity.

Processing Questions:

1. How did it feel to get a "no?"
2. How did it feel to get a "yes" or "okay?"
3. What kinds of pressure did you feel?
4. Did you find yourself ever not concentrating?
5. How does this apply to real life situations (sports, school, family, and friends)?

70A Checker Board Challenge

Example:

1. Teams have 3 minutes to discuss strategies for figuring out and remembering the correct pattern, and for deciding who goes first, second and so forth.

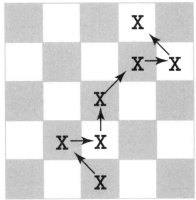

2. When the game begins, teams **can not talk or communicate** in any way with each other.

3. The choices for correct movement will always be forward, diagonally forward, or sideways.

4. Each player must have a turn before someone can go again.

5. The leader will "buzz" you if you step on an incorrect square. If you are "buzzed," you must move back to a safe square and then some-one else takes a turn.

6. The time limit for the whole game is **7 minutes**.

7. The object is to get the whole team across the board using the correct squares, but only one can be on the board at a time.

The leader picks one of these patterns and keeps it secret.

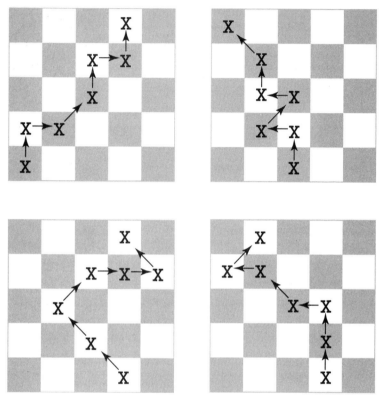

Take Five Questions: (5 minutes)

1. Share stories about the game. (fun stuff, you can talk now)
2. What was frustrating about the rules? Why?
3. What was good about the rules? Why?
4. If you could play again, would you change anything?
5. What is important about choosing the right strategy?
6. How could you relate what you learned to real life problems?

71 Pledge of Allegiance

Activity Type: Initiative

Group Size: Any size, even large assemblies

Materials: Pledge of Allegiance sheet (#71A)

Time: 5 to 10 minutes

Procedure: This is a presentation that takes the Pledge of Allegiance and divides it into parts based on the words in the text. We all know the words, but this activity adds meaning to the act of saying the pledge.

The Pledge is divided into 13 parts. Select a student volunteer for each part. Ask the volunteers to step forward one by one and say their word or phrase and it's definition. After all of the parts are said, ask the remainder or audience to stand and say the pledge as a group.

This activity involves a number of students and gives meaning to something that is important to all.

71A Pledge of Allegiance

I—   me, an individual, a committee of one.

PLEDGE—dedicate all of my worldly goods to live without pity.

ALLEGIANCE—my love and devotion.

TO THE FLAG—our standard; old glory; a symbol of freedom; whereever it waves, there's respect because your loyalty has give it a dignity that shouts freedom is everybody's job.

OF THE UNITED—that means we have all come together

STATES—individual communities that have united into 50 great states. 50 individual communities with pride and dignity and purpose. All divided with imaginary boundaries, yet unite to a common purpose and that is love for our country.

AND TO THE REPUBLIC—republic, a state in which sovereign power is invested in representatives chosen by the people to govern and government is the people. It's from the people to the leaders, not from the leaders to the people.

FOR WHICH IT STANDS—a great and united country.

ONE NATION UNDER GOD—meaning so blessed in many ways.

INDIVISIBLE—incapable of being divided.

WITH LIBERTY—which is freedom. The right of power to live one's own life without threats or fears of some sort of retaliation.

AND JUSTICE—the principles or qualities of dealing fairly with others.

FOR ALL—for all, which means, it is as much your country as it is mine.

Please stand and join us in reciting the Pledge of Allegiance.

Energizer Olson Presentations

663 Clardell Drive
Sun Prairie, Wisconsin 53590

Ph.: 608-318-0307 Fax: 608-318-0308

www.energizerolson.com
carl@energizerolson.com

Energetic, Informative, Inspirational
" Message with Magic"

I. Speaking Engagements:

Keynote addresses	Lunch/dinner speeches
Student lyceums	Convention breakouts
Training sessions	Workshop presentations
Corporate groups	Youth groups
Government offices	Health care personnel
Graduations	Awards banquets

All ages and any size group—we work with you to design the most effective presentation.

Topics Include:

Leadership, Character, Team Building, Communications, Problem Solving, Customer Service, Self-improvement, Education Activities, A.O.D.A. issues, and more.

II. Teaching & Training Supplies:

E.O.P. stocks and markets products for use in effective presentations. These products have been tried and tested with all types of groups. Products include high quality books, user-friendly magic tricks, and training manipulatives. All items are reasonably priced and relate to activities presented in the E.O.P. books. See www.energizerolson.com for ordering information.

"Make it big, do it right, give it class, and wrap it with love."

P.T. Barnum

Carl Olson

About the Author:
Carl *"Energizer"* Olson

Carl Olson is a life long educator and advocate for the experiential learning theory.

Carl's professional background includes a master's degree in education from Minnesota State University at Winona and a master's degree in guidance and counseling from Wisconsin State University—Stout. He also has experience and certification as a school administrator K-12. In addition, Carl has over 30 years of involvement in leadership education. This comes from his work as a student council adviser, Wisconsin Association of School Councils board member, leadership camp director, and presenter at various conferences and workshops. On the national level, Carl served as an adviser for the National Association of School Councils Leadership Training Center.

Resource List

Boyte, P., Jacobson, M., and Jones, R. (1997). *Focus.* Meadow Vista, CA: Learning for Living, Inc.

Butler, S. and Rohnke, K. (1995). *Quicksilver.* Dubuque, Iowa: Kendall/Hunt Publishing.

Fleugelman, A. (ed.). (1978). *The new games book.* Tiburon, CA: Headlands Press.

Fleugelman, A. (ed.). (1981). *More new games!* Tiburon, CA: Headlands Press.

Foster, E. (1989). *Energizers and icebreakers for all ages and stages.* Minneapolis, MN: Educational Media Corporation.

Foster-Harrison, E. (1994). *More Energizers and icebreakers for all ages and stages book II*. Minneapolis, MN: Educational Media Corporation.

Harris, F. (1962). *Great games to play with groups*. Torrance, CA: Frank Schaffer Pub. Inc.

Hazouri, S.P., & McLaughlin, M.S. (1993). *Warm ups & wind downs: 101 activities for moving and motivating groups*. Minneapolis, MN: Educational Media Corporation.

Jackson, T. (1993). *Activities That Teac. Cedar City, UT:* Red Rock Publishing Co.

Jackson, T. (1995). *More Activities That Teac. Cedar City, UT:* Red Rock Publishing Co.

Jacobs, M., and Turk, B. (1996). *Building a positive self-concept*. Portland ME. Weston Walch Pub.

Jefferys, M. (1989). *Speaking with magic*. New York, N.Y: Powerful Magic Press.

LeFevre, D.N. (1988). *New games for the whole family*. New York, NY: Putnam Publishing Co.

McBride, William. (1997). *Entertaining an elephant*. San Francisco, CA: First Pearl Street Press.

Orlick, T. (1978). *The cooperation sports and games book*. New York, NY: Pantheon Books.

Riedel, P.H. (1999). *Getting started: 100 icebreakers for youth gatherings*. Dayton, OH: Hi-Time Pflaum.

Rohnke, K. (1991). *The bottomless bag*. Dubuque, Iowa: Kendall/Hunt Publishing.

Rohnke, K. (1989). *Cowstails and cobras II*. Dubuque, Iowa: Kendall/Hunt Publishing.

Rohnke, K. (1984). *Silver Bullets*. Dubuque, Iowa: Kendall/Hunt Publishing.

Weinstein, M., and Goodman, J. (1980). *Playfair*. San Luis Obispo, CA: Impact Publishers.

Wenc, C.C. (1993). *Cooperation: Learning through laughter*, (second edition). Minneapolis, MN: Educational Media Corporation.